Crabs

Text by Mary Jo Rhodes and David Hall
Photographs by David Hall

Undersea Encounters

Children's Press®
A Division of Scholastic Inc.
New York   Toronto   London   Auckland   Sydney
Mexico City   New Delhi   Hong Kong
Danbury, Connecticut

Library of Congress Cataloging-in-Publication Data

Rhodes, Mary Jo, 1957–
    Crabs / text by Mary Jo Rhodes and David Hall; photographs by David Hall.
        p. cm. (Undersea encounters)
    Includes index.
    ISBN-10: 0-516-24390-X (lib. bdg.)   0-516-25354-9 (pbk.)
    ISBN-13: 978-0-516-24390-0 (lib. bdg.)   978-0-516-25354-1 (pbk.)
    1. Crabs—Juvenile literature. I. Hall, David, 1943 Oct. 2– II. Title.
III. Series: Rhodes, Mary Jo, 1957–
    QL444.M33R56 2006
    595.3'86—dc22
                                        2005024565

*To my young diving companions whose enthusiasm helped inspire this series: Jamie, Jessica,
Aron, Noah, Daniel, Maya, Jenny, and Becky.
—D.H.
To the memory of my mother, Toby Kennedy, for all the wonderful times we spent together near
our favorite place—the ocean. And to the memory of my stepfather, Donald Stewart Kennedy,
who taught me how to swim in the ocean.
—M.J.R.*

All photographs © 2007 by David Hall except: Corbis Images/Renee Lynn: 16 bottom;
Maris Kazmers: 23 top; Minden Pictures/Fred Bavendam: 34; National Geographic Image
Collection/George Grall: 10; Nature Picture Library Ltd./Pete Oxford: 42; Visuals
Unlimited/Wim van Egmond: 36.

A decorator crab wears a living costume.
pg. **30**

Crabs

The boxer crab carries stinging animals in its claws.
pg. **25**

Hermit crabs live inside old snail shells.
pg. **38**

Up close a crab looks like an
alien visitor from another world.

chapter 1

What Is a Crab?

A crab may seem like an alien visitor from another world. It walks on many legs. It is covered with heavy armor and has weapons for crushing or cutting its enemies. Its eyes are on stalks that stick up from its head. Yet crabs are closely related to much more familiar animals. In fact, some of their relatives are probably living in your house!

Legs with Joints

Like snails or worms, crabs are invertebrates—animals without a backbone. They belong to the largest invertebrate group, the **arthropods**. Arthropods have a hard outer covering, or **exoskeleton**, and legs that bend at joints. Arthropods include many familiar animals such as insects and spiders.

Like crabs, spiders have legs that bend at joints. Crabs and spiders are arthropods.

Crabs, along with lobsters and shrimps, belong to the group of arthropods known as **crustaceans**. Like insects, crustaceans' bodies have three sections: head, **thorax**, and **abdomen**. Unlike insects, a crustacean's head and thorax are joined tightly together and seem like one section. In addition, crustaceans have two pairs of **antennae** while insects have just one pair.

Lobsters are closely related to crabs. Both have three body sections and two pairs of feelers, or antennae.

Crustaceans also have gills for breathing underwater and insects do not.

True and False Crabs

There are two kinds of crabs. True crabs, or **brachyurans**, have a very short abdomen and use four pairs of long legs for walking. Blue

This squat lobster is a false crab. Unlike a true crab, it has only three pairs of long walking legs and an abdomen that is easily visible.

crabs, spider crabs, and ghost crabs are all true crabs. False crabs, or **anomurans**, have a longer abdominal section and fewer walking legs. False crabs include hermit crabs, king crabs, and squat lobsters.

Feeling, Tasting, and Seeing

Crabs have two pairs of antennae. They can touch, smell, and taste with their antennae. Crabs also have hair-like bristles on the outside of their bodies. The bristles help them feel nearby objects and sense the movement of the water.

Crab Fact

Horseshoe crabs are arthropods, but they are not really crabs or even crustaceans. Their closest living relatives are spiders.

Crabs' eyes are on the ends of stalks. Crabs have large compound eyes made up of hundreds of tiny lenses. Compound eyes are especially good for spotting movement. They help crabs to find prey and to spot approaching **predators**.

The eyes of a crab are on the ends of long stalks. Each eye is made up of hundreds of small lenses.

Limbs for Different Purposes

A true crab has eight pairs of limbs attached to its body. These include four pairs of walking or swimming legs and one pair of legs with claws, the **chelipeds**. In addition, three pairs of **maxillipeds** near the mouth are used for feeding.

A crab's claws are remarkable tools. They can be used like a vise for crushing or like scissors for cutting. They can also be used like chopsticks for catching fish or picking up food.

Parts of a Blue Crab

cheliped with claw

two pairs of antennae

legs bend at joints

eyes on stalks

rear legs paddle-shaped
for swimming

carapace covers head and thorax
(short abdomen hidden underneath)

True crabs have four pairs of legs used for walking and a short abdomen hidden beneath their body. Their bodies are covered by a hard shell called a **carapace**. The paddle-shaped rear legs of this blue crab can also be used for swimming. Its front pair of walking legs are not visible in this photograph.

The rear walking legs of some true crabs, called swimming crabs, are shaped like paddles. These flattened legs can be used for both walking and swimming.

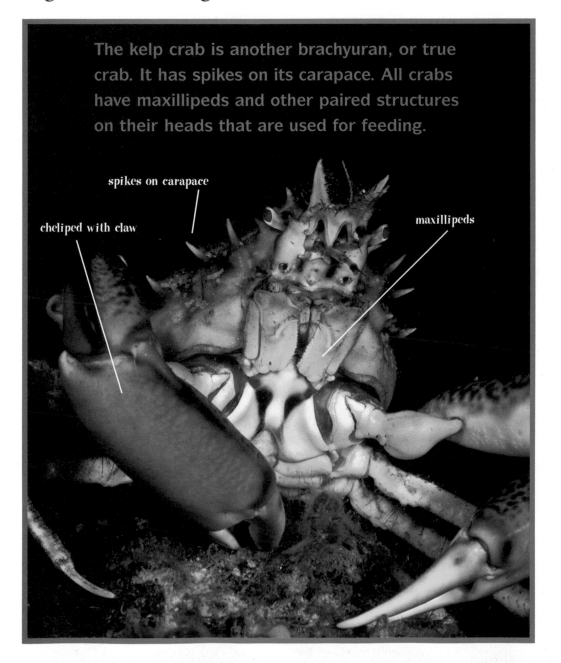

The kelp crab is another brachyuran, or true crab. It has spikes on its carapace. All crabs have maxillipeds and other paired structures on their heads that are used for feeding.

spikes on carapace

cheliped with claw

maxillipeds

The chirostylid, or deep sea squat lobster, is a false crab that can be found on soft corals. Chirostylids live mostly at great depths, so not much is known about them.

chapter 2

Where Do Crabs Live?

Crabs are found almost everywhere in the ocean. They live near smoking volcanic vents thousands of feet below the surface. They live under the ice in Antarctica. You will find them where huge waves crash on rocky shores. One type of crab even lives on land and climbs trees. Crabs live in more different places than any other sea animal.

Rocks and Seaweed

Some crabs live on rocky sea bottoms near the shore. Cancer crabs and long-legged spider crabs commonly feed among the rocks and seaweed. (Cancer is a scientific name that means "crab" in Latin.)

Like many crabs, cancer crabs aren't picky eaters. They are **scavengers**. This means that they eat dead or decaying plants and animals. Some are also predators that hunt and eat snails, worms, and other small animals.

The Jonah crab, a typical cancer crab, lives on rocky sea bottoms in cold North Atlantic waters.

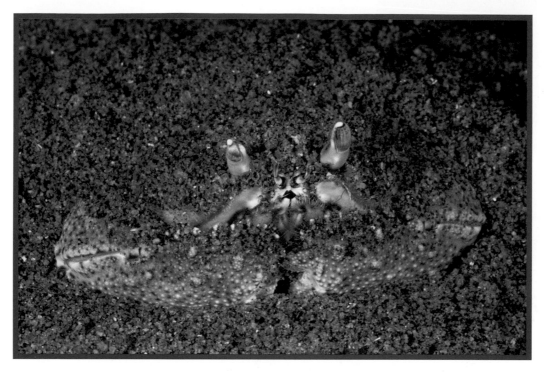

Box crabs live on sandy sea bottoms. They often bury themselves to hide from enemies.

A Sandy Seafloor

Swimming crabs, box crabs, and pebble crabs live on sand or mud sea bottoms. Their pale colors help them blend in, making them difficult to see. Swimming crabs are fast-moving predators. They hunt and eat invertebrates and even small fish. Box crabs and pebble crabs spend the day hidden under the sand. They come out at night to scavenge for food.

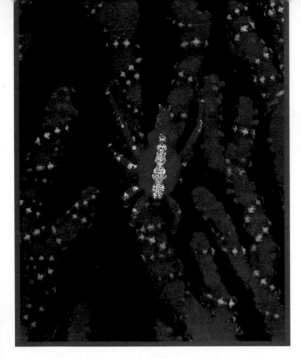

This tiny spider crab is the same color as the coral on which it lives.

Coral Reefs

Tropical coral reefs provide homes for many kinds of crabs. Tiny xanthid (ZAN-thid) and trapeze (tra-PEEZ) crabs live among hard coral branches. Spider crabs often live on soft corals.

Rocky Shores

Shore crabs live where waves break on rocky shores. Many of them are intertidal animals. This means that they live between

The Sally Lightfoot crab is a shore crab. It lives where waves break on rocky shores.

the high and low tide watermarks on the shore. Many shore crabs live and breathe both underwater and on land.

Fast-moving ghost crabs live on sandy beaches. This female crab is carrying thousands of orange eggs under her belly.

Sandy Beaches

Ghost crabs and fiddler crabs live out of the water along sandy or muddy shores. Ghost crabs are fierce predators that attack hatchling sea turtles and shorebird chicks. Fiddler crab males have one claw that is much larger than the other. It is used for combat with other males and for attracting a mate.

Crab Fact

True crabs can walk slowly in any direction, but when they need to hurry, they usually move sideways.

Living with a Partner

Small crabs sometimes live with a "big brother" for protection. Many of these animal partners have sharp spines or stingers that can help protect the crab. The partner may provide the crab with free transportation. It may also help the crab find food. Corals, **sea anemones**, sea urchins, and sea cucumbers are common crab partners.

This swimming crab makes its home on a sea cucumber, a large, wormlike sea star relative.

Pea crabs are the smallest of all crabs. This one lives among the spines of a sea urchin.

Porcelain crabs live with sea anemones and other animals. Their netlike mouthparts capture bits of food from the water.

The zebra crab's color pattern makes it hard to see among the stinging spines of a fire urchin.

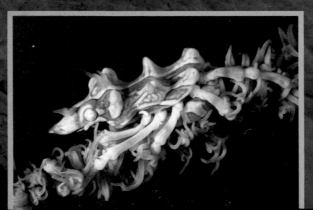

A xeno crab blends in with branches of the wire coral on which it lives.

A small black coral crab spreads its claws wide apart when threatened. This defensive reaction makes the crab appear larger.

chapter 3

Enemies and Defenses

What do people, loggerhead sea turtles, fish, octopuses, sea lions, and shorebirds all have in common? They all enjoy a crab dinner! Because crabs taste so good, they must defend themselves against all of the animals that would like to eat them.

A Safe Place to Hide

With their flat bodies, crabs can squeeze into tight spaces where predators can't easily reach them. Crabs may

A pair of tiny trapeze crabs is safe among hard coral branches. Most predators are unable to squeeze into such tight places.

hide among coral branches or under rocks. Some crabs even hide inside sponges or old barnacle shells.

Armor and Claws

Crabs have a strong protective shell that is like a suit of armor. But this does not stop predators such as large fish, seals, and sea turtles. These animals have powerful jaws that can easily break through the shell.

Crabs also have an active defense: their claws. A crab may wave its claws around to look bigger and more threatening. If that doesn't work, the crab may

Crab Fact

Most crabs can fit in the palm of your hand. But one deepwater spider crab is a giant. Its legs can be up to 6 feet (2 meters) long.

A small crab uses its claws to defend itself against a fish.

use its claws to deliver a painful pinch.

The large claws of a box crab fit tightly in front of the crab's head. Its claws are like a thick door that closes tightly, protecting the crab from danger.

A box crab hides behind its claws, using them like a shield.

This hermit crab places stinging sea anemones on its shell to discourage predators. Each time the crab moves into a larger shell, it transfers the anemones to its new home.

When its other defenses fail, a crab has one last trick. If a large fish or other predator grabs it by a leg, the leg will often break off. The crab can then scramble away on its other legs. Over time, the lost leg will grow back as good as new.

Live Weapons

Some crabs use sea anemones as living weapons. A hermit crab may place anemones on its borrowed shell, or a decorator crab may place them on its carapace. The tiny boxer crab carries a pair of stinging anemones in its claws. Any predator that threatens these crabs will get stung. In return, the anemones get free transportation.

A boxer crab defends itself with stinging sea anemones. It carries one anemone in each claw.

Can you see the small crab hidden among the soft coral branches? This decorator crab disguises itself by wearing bits of live coral on its shell.

chapter 4

Crabs in Disguise

A predator can't catch what it doesn't see. Some crabs blend in so well with their surroundings that they are almost invisible to predators. Decorator crabs disguise themselves by wearing costumes made of other animals and live plants. The plants and animals worn for disguise include seaweeds, sponges, and sea anemones.

When threatened, the stealth crab remains very still and plays dead.

Hidden Crabs

Certain crabs have a shape or color that makes them hard to recognize. The stealth crab has a large white carapace that resembles an old clam shell. When threatened, the crab plays dead by holding very still. This act seems to fool most predators.

Some crabs have the same color pattern as their surroundings. The banded anemone crab takes on a pale color when it lives with white soft coral. The color pattern of certain small spider crabs closely matches the appearance of the branching coral on which they live.

The color pattern of this banded anemone crab blends in with the coral animals around it.

A Sponge Hat

A crab's natural color doesn't always work to hide it. A sponge crab hides by wearing a sponge on its back. This "living hat" is held in place by the crab's back legs. When no sponges are handy, the crab may use sea squirts or seaweeds to cover itself. If you are underwater and see a walking sponge, you are probably looking at a sponge crab!

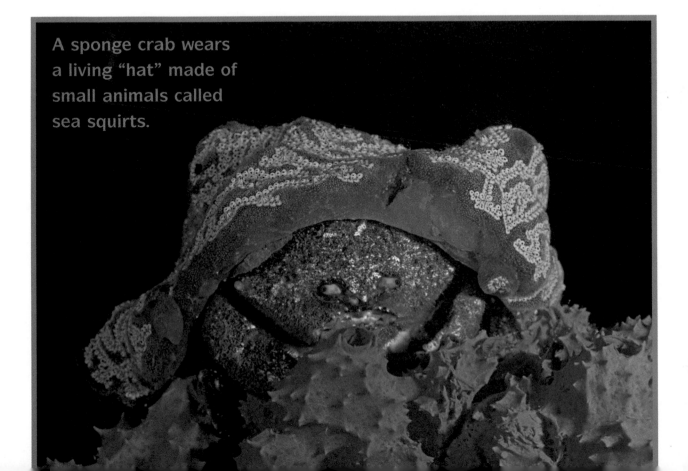

A sponge crab wears a living "hat" made of small animals called sea squirts.

Decorator Crabs

Some spider crabs disguise themselves by attaching living things to their bodies. These are held in place by small spikes on the crab's shell. The crab on this page has disguised itself with a sea anemone, bits of green seaweed, and several different sponges.

Living decorations do more than just disguise a crab. Sponges have a bad taste that predators don't like. Anemones have stingers that discourage predators.

Hidden among pink soft corals, this crab is also disguised by the red seaweed attached to its shell.

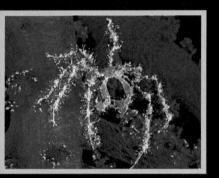

Dozens of tiny stinging hydroids cover the exoskeleton of this small decorator crab.

The orangutan crab gets its hairy appearance from simple plants known as red algae.

This crab has completely covered itself with bits of sponge and other living things.

A male rock crab mates with a smaller female. He will stay attached to her for several days.

chapter 5

Growing and Mating

Living inside a suit of armor isn't always easy. The outer shell of a crab protects and supports it, but does cause some problems. Growth is one problem. If your skin won't stretch, how can you grow larger? The hard outer shell also makes mating difficult. Fortunately, crabs have developed a way around these problems. It is called molting.

Molting

From time to time, a crab outgrows its exoskeleton, or "shell." It must molt, or replace its old shell with a larger one. A crab may molt dozens of times during its life. It molts most often when it is young and growing rapidly.

When a crab needs to molt, a new exoskeleton begins forming beneath the old one. The old shell splits open, and the crab climbs out of it. While its new shell is soft, the crab has little protection. It will usually hide for a few days until the shell hardens.

A crab (right) has just shed its old exoskeleton (left). This is called molting.

Finding a Mate

A female crab may be ready to mate when she is one to two years old. Mating can only take place shortly after the female has molted. She releases a substance called a pheromone into the water to attract a male. When the male finds her, he gives her a "hug"

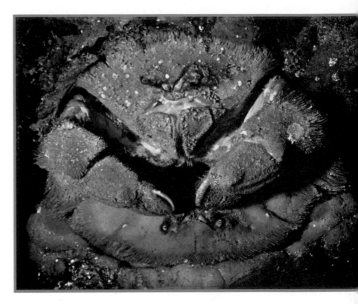

A male sponge crab protects his mate until her new shell has hardened.

that may last for several days. By holding her close, he keeps other males away and protects her from predators until her new shell hardens. During this time, the male's **sperm** passes into the female's body.

Crab Fact

Soft-shelled crab is served in many seafood restaurants. A crab is soft-shelled after it has shed its old shell and before the new one has hardened.

Crab Larvae

Crabs hatch as tiny larvae (LAR-vee) the size of the head of a pin. Just as caterpillars look different from butterflies, crab larvae look different from adult crabs. Crab larvae float for several weeks before settling to the ocean floor.

This newly hatched crab, known as a zoea larva, looks very different from its parents.

This female crab has millions of orange eggs attached to her belly. She will carry the eggs around until they hatch.

Millions of Eggs

When the female lays her eggs, the male's sperm will **fertilize** them. Female crabs may lay several million eggs at one time. The orange eggs, covered with a sticky substance, cling together in a large clump. The female carries them underneath her body until the eggs hatch.

A hermit crab lives inside an old
snail shell to protect its soft body.

chapter 6

Hermit Crabs

Hermit crabs are false crabs, or anomurans. Unlike true crabs, hermits have a long, soft abdomen that must be protected. Like a true crab, a hermit crab has ten legs, with claws on the two front legs. Unlike a true crab, a hermit crab doesn't use all of its remaining legs for walking.

A Mobile Home

To protect the rear part of its body, a hermit crab lives inside an empty snail

A large hermit crab threatens a smaller one. The smaller crab has retreated deep inside its borrowed shell.

This hermit crab is about to try on a new shell to see if it fits better than the old one.

shell. The crab holds on to the inside of the shell with two pairs of tiny rear legs.

Hermit crabs live in many different kinds of snail shells. The shell must be the right size and shape and be in good condition. When threatened, a hermit crab retreats into its shell. It may try to cover the opening with one or both claws.

House Hunting

As a hermit crab grows, it needs to move into a larger "house" from time to time. First, it must find an empty shell that is about the right size. Then it lets go of its old shell and quickly moves into the new one. If the new shell fits properly, the crab will stay there.

Empty shells can be scarce. Sometimes two or more hermit crabs will fight over one shell.

Unusual Hermit Homes

Coral hermit crabs live in small holes in hard coral. These crabs do not leave their holes to search for food. They wave their feathery antennae to catch tiny floating plants and animals.

The miner hermit crab lives inside a small rock or broken piece of coral that it carries around. The crab creates a hole or enlarges an existing hole until it can fit inside the rock. As it grows, the miner crab enlarges the hole.

Coral hermit crabs have homes that they cannot carry with them. They live inside old wormholes in hard coral.

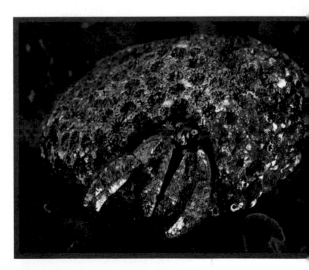

A miner hermit crab lives inside a small piece of soft rock.

The coconut crab may climb a tree in search of coconuts to eat.

A Giant Land Hermit

The coconut crab is a giant hermit crab. It lives on islands in the Pacific Ocean and the Indian Ocean. Weighing up to 10 pounds (4 kilograms), it is the world's largest land invertebrate.

Like other hermit crabs, a coconut crab begins its life in the ocean. When it is young, it lives in old snail shells. Eventually, it becomes so big that it no longer needs a snail shell for protection. Coconut crabs are scavengers, but they also eat fresh fruit. They will even climb palm trees in search of a meal.

Hermit Crabs As Pets

Land hermit crabs make excellent pets. With proper care, they can live for many years. Being scavengers, they aren't fussy eaters. Hermit crabs need a crabarium, an enclosed crab habitat, stocked with empty shells that they can move into. They also need branches to climb on and some soft material to hide in when molting. By taking care of a hermit crab, you can learn a lot about these interesting crustaceans.

This unusual hermit crab has a very flat body. It is able to fit into the narrow space inside a cone snail shell.

Glossary

abdomen (**AB-duh-min**) belly; the rear section of a crab's body
(pg. 6)

anomurans (**an-o-MUR-anz**) crustaceans, such as hermit crabs, also
called false crabs; anomurans have a longer abdomen and fewer walking
legs than true crabs *(pg. 8)*

antennae (**an-TEN-ee**) a pair of thin, flexible organs on the head of
an insect or crustacean used for sensing its surroundings *(pg. 6)*

arthropods (**AR-thruh-podz**) animals with jointed legs, a body
divided into two or more parts, and an outer skeleton *(pg. 6)*

brachyurans (**brake-ee-YUR-uhnz**) the scientific name for true crabs;
crustaceans with claws, four pairs of walking legs, and a short abdomen
curled tightly underneath the body *(pg. 7)*

carapace (**KARE-uh-pace**) the thick shell covering a crab's head and
thorax *(pg. 10)*

chelipeds (**KEE-luh-pedz**) a crab's front limbs that end in claws *(pg. 9)*

crustaceans (**kruhss-TAY-shuhnz**) arthropods with two pairs of
antennae and a body with three parts; most live in the ocean *(pg. 6)*

exoskeleton (eks-oh-SKEL-uh-tuhn) the hard outer covering of an arthropod's body; it is attached to the muscles and provides protection and support *(pg. 6)*

fertilize (FER-tuhl-ize) to provide sperm to join with an egg and produce young *(pg. 37)*

maxillipeds (max-ILL-uh-pedz) pairs of limbs on the head of a crab, used for passing food to its mouth *(pg. 9)*

predators (PRED-uh-turz) animals that hunt and kill other animals for food *(pg. 9)*

scavengers (SKAV-uhnj-urz) animals that feed on dead or decaying animals or plants *(pg. 14)*

sea anemones (SEE uh-NEM-uh-nees) stinging animals related to corals and jellyfish *(pg. 18)*

sperm (SPURM) cells from a male animal that can fertilize the eggs of a female of the same species *(pg. 35)*

thorax (THOR-ax) the middle section of a crustacean's body *(pg. 6)*

Learn More About Crabs

Books

Binns, Tristan Boyer. *Hermit Crabs.* Chicago: Heinemann Library, 2004.

Blaxland, Beth. *Crabs, Crayfishes, and Their Relatives.* Broomall, Pa.: Chelsea House, 2002.

Greenaway, Theresa, and Colin Newman (illustrator). *The Secret World of Crabs.* Austin, Tex.: Raintree Steck-Vaughn, 2001.

Web Sites

Crab General Biology—Museum Victoria Australia
http://www.museum.vic.gov.au/crust/crabbiol.html

Mystic Aquarium—Ocean Animals
http://www.mysticaquarium.org

Smithsonian Environmental Research Center—Blue Crab Online Resource
http://www.serc.si.edu/education/resources/bluecrab/index.jsp

Smithsonian National Zoological Park: Land Hermit Crab
http://nationalzoo.si.edu/Animals/ThinkTank/Animals/LandHermitCrab/default.cfm

Index

47

About the Authors

With degrees in zoology and medicine, **David Hall** has worked for the past twenty-five years as both a wildlife photojournalist and a physician. His articles and photographs have appeared in hundreds of calendars, books, and magazines, including *National Geographic, Smithsonian, Natural History*, and *Ranger Rick*. His underwater images have won many major awards, including Nature's Best, BBC Wildlife Photographer of the Year, and Festival Mondial de l'Image Sous-Marine. To see more of David's work, visit www.seaphotos.com.

Mary Jo Rhodes received her master's degree in library service from Columbia University and was a librarian for the Brooklyn Public Library. She later worked for ten years in children's book publishing in New York City. Mary Jo lives with her husband, John Rounds, and teenage sons, Jeremy and Tim, in Hoboken, New Jersey. Mary Jo learned a lot about crustacean behavior from her family's pet hermit crab, which lived for eleven years. To learn more about Mary Jo Rhodes and her books, visit www.maryjorhodes.com.

About the Consultant

Karen Gowlett-Holmes, one of Australia's leading marine biologists, is a recognized expert on the classification of mollusks and other marine invertebrates. She has worked as Collection Manager of Marine Invertebrates for the South Australia Museum and for Australia's scientific and industrial research organization, CSIRO. Karen has written a number of popular articles and book chapters, and has published more than forty scientific papers.